That can't be true?

Written by Simon Yeend

Collins

Be an animal detective!

Animals have remarkable survival skills, some that you may struggle to believe are true.

True or False

- Wood frogs freeze solid to get through icy winters … and then wake up again in spring.
- Octopuses can squeeze through the tiniest gaps to escape predators.
- Spiders will die if they lose a leg.

It's your chance to be an animal detective! Can you work out which of the wild facts on the next pages are true and which are just tall tales?

Humans have the same number of neck bones as giraffes.

True or False

True!

Giraffes only have seven neck bones, called vertebrae, which is the same as humans.

So giraffes' necks are just like ours – only much longer and the bones are bigger! A human neck is around 10 centimetres long, while a giraffe's neck can be as long as 2.4 metres.

In fact, nearly all **mammals** – from tiny mice to giant blue whales – have seven neck bones. It's amazing how animals that look so different are built the same way.

Did you know?

Giraffes give birth standing up. So the first thing a baby giraffe does is fall 1.5 metres to the ground. Thankfully, they soon recover and are standing by themselves within an hour!

False!

Hippos can't really swim at all. Instead, they sink and walk or bounce along the bottom of rivers and lakes and hold their breath when they are underwater. They can hold their breath for up to five minutes!

Did you know?

Hippos spend up to 16 hours a day in water to keep cool. They can breathe air while being almost totally submerged because their nostrils are located on the upper part of their snout.
When they dive, their nostrils slam shut, so no water gets in.

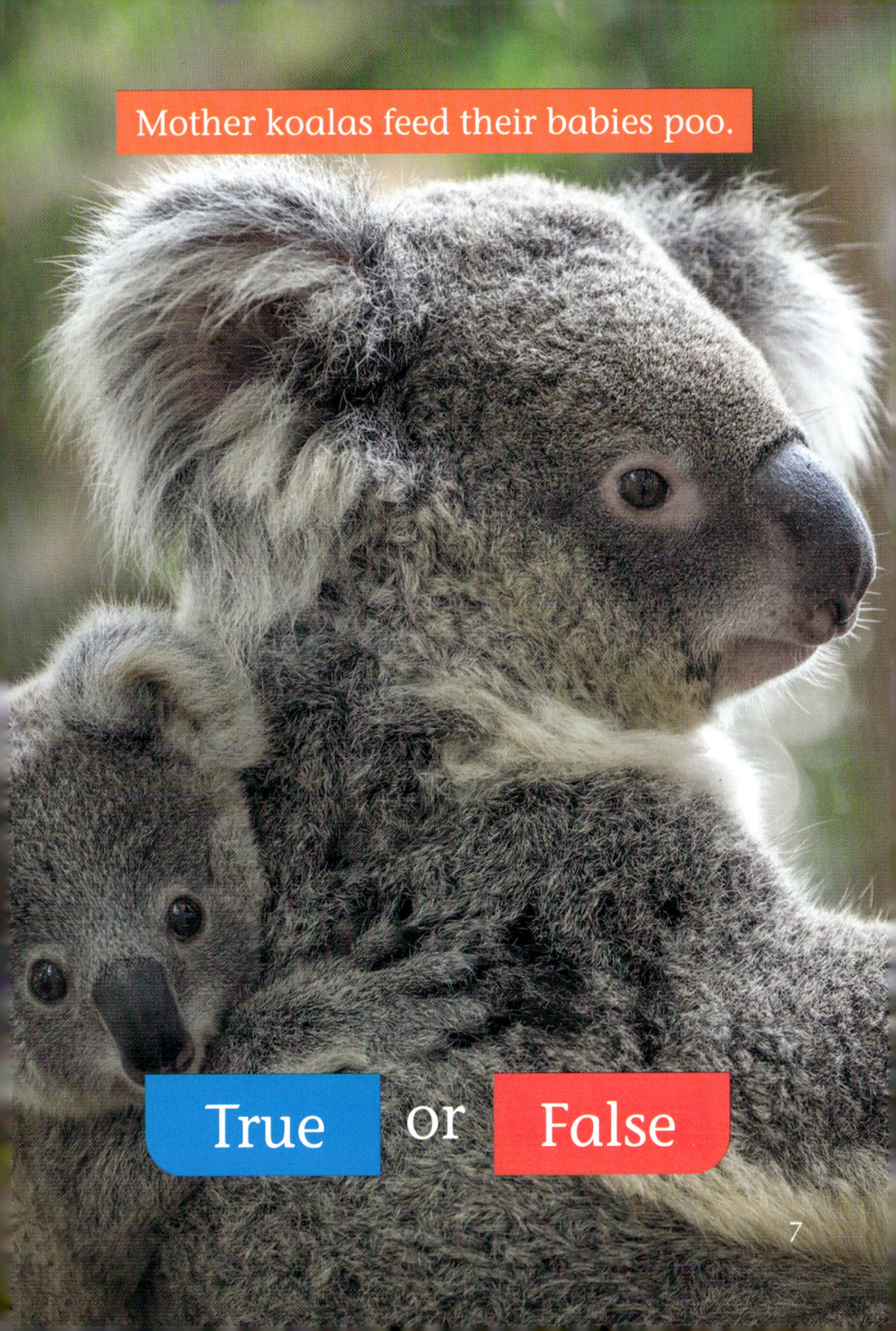

Mother koalas feed their babies poo.

True or False

True!

Koalas eat almost nothing but eucalyptus leaves, which are tough to break down and contain toxins that are dangerous to baby koalas. For the first five or six months the joey – the name for a baby – drinks only the mother's milk. Later, the mother starts to feed them a special form of their own poo – called pap. Pap is rich in gut bacteria, which allows adult koalas to detoxify and digest the leaves. By eating pap, the youngsters take in this helpful bacteria, which allows them to be able to eat eucalyptus leaves as they grow older.

Did you know?

Koalas aren't bears at all! They are **marsupials**, like kangaroos, and have pouches where their babies develop.

False!

Cats also have special whiskers on the backs of their front legs called carpal whiskers.

These whiskers work like a radar, helping cats to sense what's around them, even in the dark. They guide cats silently while they hunt and explore.

The whiskers on a cat's face act like a built-in ruler! Cats know that if their whiskers fit though a tight gap, the rest of their body will, too.

Did you know?

Cats can jump around six times their own height. That's like you leaping over a two-storey house!

Spiders will die if they lose a leg.

True or False

False!

If a spider loses a leg, it can grow a brand new one! Young spiders can sprout a new leg that will be just as strong and speedy as the first one. Adult spiders can re-grow legs too, but theirs often come back smaller or thinner.

How does this work? Spiders re-grow legs during moulting, which is when they shed their hard **exoskeleton** and grow a new one.

Did you know?

Spiders aren't the only creatures with regrowth superpowers. Starfish can grow back entire arms and lizards can drop their tails to escape predators, growing a new one later.

Foxes' eyes turn blue in the winter to help them see better in lower light levels.

True or False

False!

Foxes' eyes don't change colour in winter. But reindeer's eyes do!

In summer, the back part of their eyes is shiny gold to help protect them from strong sunlight, like wearing sunglasses.

In winter, the same part of the eye turns blue to help them see better in the dark. Their eyes don't look blue from the outside, though – it's like a secret change happening inside their eyes!

Did you know?

Reindeer are unique among all the deer species, because both males and females grow **antlers**.

An octopus can squeeze through a gap no bigger than its **beak**.

True or False

True!

Octopuses are the ocean's squishy escape artists! With no bones to hold them back, they can wriggle through the tiniest spaces to escape predators.

Their bodies are like soft, stretchy slime. The only hard part is their beak, sitting right in the middle of their arms. So, if their beak fits, the rest of their body can, too! It's like they melt through the tiniest gaps, flowing like water.

octopus beak

Did you know?

Octopuses can taste with their arms! Imagine touching your favourite snack and knowing exactly how it tastes without even taking a bite!

Wood frogs can freeze solid ... and survive!

True or False

True!

To survive freezing temperatures, wood frogs use a super-cool trick. They produce sugary antifreeze in their liver. This **glucose** syrup stops ice from forming inside their cells, so only the spaces around them freeze. Then their hearts stop and they even stop breathing!

When spring comes, the weather warms up. The frog starts to melt – from the inside out! The heart melts first and then its other organs and muscles, until the frog is ready to hop back to life.

Did you know?

Frogs don't drink water like most other animals. Instead, they soak it up through their skin like a sponge!

Bats have terrible eyesight.

True or False

False!

Bats have pretty good eyesight. During the day, they use their eyes to find food, explore and avoid obstacles – just like us!

At night, bats unleash their superpower: **echolocation**! They send out squeaky sounds that bounce off objects around them, even tiny bugs. When the sounds bounce back, bats can "hear" exactly where those objects are.

Did you know?

The Mexican free-tailed bat can fly faster than a car – up to 160 kilometres per hour. That makes it the fastest mammal in the world!

Male gentoo penguins try to attract a female by singing to her.

True or False

False!

Male gentoo penguins don't sing – they bring pebbles hoping to attract a mate. The male carefully selects the perfect pebble, scoops it up in his beak, and waddles over to his partner.

If the female likes the pebble, she'll accept it – and the penguins pair up!

Together they build a cosy nest out of pebbles for their two eggs and team up to care for their chicks.

Did you know?

Penguins' black and white colouring is actually camouflage, protecting them from predators in the water.
From above, their black backs blend into the deep ocean. From below, their white bellies look like the bright surface of the sea.

Ostriches bury their heads in the sand when they are scared.

True or False

False!

The idea that ostriches bury their heads is just a myth. Ostriches can't fly, so, instead of building a nest in a tree, they dig shallow holes for their eggs. From time to time, they lower their heads to turn the eggs, which might look like they are burying their heads.

Also, when ostriches sense danger, they lie flat to hide, which also looks like they are burying their heads.

Did you know?

Ostriches lay the world's largest eggs! Each one weighs as much as 20 chicken eggs – about 1.4 kilogrammes!

When it's cold, red pandas use their tails as a blanket to keep warm.

True or False

True!

Red pandas do use their long, bushy tails as a blanket when sleeping. They live in the **Himalayas** and mountain ranges of China where winters can be bitterly cold.

A red panda's tail is longer than its body (up to 47 centimetres) and is extremely fluffy. When they sleep in trees, red pandas often curl up into a tight ball with their tail wrapped over their face to protect them from the cold mountain air.

Did you know?

Red pandas have fur on the soles of their paws. This helps them grip icy branches and provides insulation from snow – like built-in snow boots!

After reading all these animal facts and myths, which animals do you want to know more about? Which was your favourite fact? And your favourite myth?

Glossary

antlers   branch-like horns on deer

beak   the scissor-like mouth of an octopus

echolocation   special sounds that bats make, which bounce back to help them "see" in the dark

exoskeleton   a spider's hard outer shell, which protects its body

glucose   a natural sugar that gives animals and plants energy

Himalayas   a mountain range in Asia

mammals   warm-blooded animals with fur or hair that feed their babies milk

marsupials   animals that carry their babies in pouches, such as kangaroos

Index

bat 19–20

cat 9–10

fox 13–14

giraffe 3–4

hippos 5–6

koala 7–8

octopus 15–16

ostrich 23–24

penguin 21–22

red panda 25–26

reindeer 14

spider 11–12

wood frog 17–18

29

Which ones were true?

 gives birth standing up

 fantastic swimmer

 is a marsupial

 only has whiskers on its face

 can lose a tail and grow a new one

eyes change colour to blue in winter

can squeeze through tiny gaps

drinks water through its skin

great at underwater camouflage

buries its head in the sand when scared

Ideas for reading

Written by Gill Matthews
Primary Literacy Consultant

Reading objectives:
- be introduced to non-fiction books that are structured in different ways
- discuss and clarify the meanings of words, linking new meanings to known vocabulary
- draw on what they already know or on background information and vocabulary provided by the teacher
- answer and ask questions

Spoken language objectives:
- articulate and justify answers, arguments and opinions
- participate in discussions, presentations, performances, role play, improvisations and debates

Curriculum links: Science: Living things and their habitats

Interest words: survival, escape, predators

Word count: 1447

Build a context for reading

- Ask children to look closely at the front cover of the book and to read the title. Explore their knowledge of the animals pictured on the cover.
- Discuss what they think the book might be about.
- Read the back cover blurb and talk about the question.
- Point out that this is a non-fiction book. Encourage children to talk about what they know about non-fiction books.

Understand and apply reading strategies

- Read p2 aloud. Discuss the three bullet points, encouraging children to say whether they think they are true or false. Encourage them to support their responses with opinions and reasons. Ensure children understand the term *tall tales*.
- Read p3 and ask children whether they think the statement is true or false, and why.
- Read p4. Ask children what they think is the most fascinating fact about *giraffes*.